I0020581

Instant OpenLayers Starter

Web Mapping made simple and fast!

Alessio Di Lorenzo

Giovanni Allegri

BIRMINGHAM - MUMBAI

Instant OpenLayers Starter

Copyright © 2013 Packt Publishing

All rights reserved. No part of this book may be reproduced, stored in a retrieval system, or transmitted in any form or by any means, without the prior written permission of the publisher, except in the case of brief quotations embedded in critical articles or reviews.

Every effort has been made in the preparation of this book to ensure the accuracy of the information presented. However, the information contained in this book is sold without warranty, either express or implied. Neither the authors, nor Packt Publishing, and its dealers and distributors will be held liable for any damages caused or alleged to be caused directly or indirectly by this book.

Packt Publishing has endeavored to provide trademark information about all of the companies and products mentioned in this book by the appropriate use of capitals. However, Packt Publishing cannot guarantee the accuracy of this information.

First published: April 2013

Production Reference: 1190413

Published by Packt Publishing Ltd.
Livery Place
35 Livery Street
Birmingham B3 2PB, UK.

ISBN 978-1-78216-510-1

www.packtpub.com

Credits

Authors

Alessio Di Lorenzo

Giovanni Allegri

Reviewer

Antonio Santiago

Acquisition Editor

Usha Iyer

Commissioning Editor

Neha Nagwekar

Technical Editor

Prasad Dalvi

Project Coordinator

Amigya Khurana

Proofreader

Joel T. Johnson

Production Coordinator

Melwyn Dsa

Cover Work

Melwyn Dsa

Cover Image

Abhinash Sahu

About the Authors

Alessio Di Lorenzo is a Marine Biologist and an MSc in Geographical Information Systems and Remote Sensing. Now he is living in Pescara, Italy, the place where he was born in October 1979.

One fine day, looking for suitable tools to represent and analyze the environmental phenomena, he discovered GIS and decided that it was worthwhile to investigate the topic. By mixing his personal interest in computer science, open source software, and programming languages with the spatial knowledge, he has concentrated more and more on Web Mapping and Web GIS.

Nowadays, he works as a consultant and trainer for local and central governments and various organizations. Most of his experience concerns the use of geospatial and web technologies to study and manage data from emergency and monitoring plans in the environmental, veterinary, and public health fields. He is author and co-author of articles concerning GIS for various scientific papers and for the TANTO blog.

When not having fun with maps and connected stuff, he likes to spend his time swimming and riding his mountain bike or his motorcycle!

Giovanni Allegri has a degree in Earth Science from the **Centre for Geotechnologies (CGT)** at the University of Siena (Italy). He works as a GIS freelance consultant and analyst for public agencies and private companies. His work fields range from spatial data modeling and GIS analysis, to GIS/WebGIS software development and cartography.

He holds courses on spatial DB design and management, GIS analysis, and WebGIS development, mainly based on free and open source technologies.

I want to thank my colleagues in the editorial staff of the Italian blog TANTO, for sustaining the authoring of the current work. I also want to say thanks to the OpenLayers community and the other GFOSS communities for the precious work in spreading and sharing an open knowledge for geography and geomatics.

About the Reviewer

Antonio Santiago has more than ten years of experience in Computer Science, designing and implementing systems.

Since the beginning of his professional life, his experience has always been related to the world of the meteorology, working for different companies as an employee and freelance. He is experienced in development of systems to collect, store, transform, analyze, and visualize data and is actively interested on any GIS-related technology, with preference for data visualization.

As a restless mind, which is mainly experienced in the Java ecosystem, he also has worked actively with many related web technologies. He is always looking to improve the client side of web applications.

He is a firm believer of Software Engineering practices. He is an enthusiast of agile methodologies involving customers as a main key for the project's success.

Antonio is also the author of the *OpenLayers Cookbook* by *Packt Publishing*.

www.packtpub.com

Support files, eBooks, discount offers and more

You might want to visit www.packtpub.com for support files and downloads related to your book.

Did you know that Packt offers eBook versions of every book published, with PDF and ePub files available? You can upgrade to the eBook version at www.packtpub.com and as a print book customer, you are entitled to a discount on the eBook copy. Get in touch with us at service@packtpub.com for more details.

At www.packtpub.com, you can also read a collection of free technical articles, sign up for a range of free newsletters and receive exclusive discounts and offers on Packt books and eBooks.

packtlib.packtpub.com

Do you need instant solutions to your IT questions? PacktLib is Packt's online digital book library. Here, you can access, read and search across Packt's entire library of books.

Why Subscribe?

- ✦ Fully searchable across every book published by Packt
- ✦ Copy and paste, print and bookmark content
- ✦ On demand and accessible via web browser

Free Access for Packt account holders

If you have an account with Packt at www.packtpub.com, you can use this to access PacktLib today and view nine entirely free books. Simply use your login credentials for immediate access.

Table of Contents

Instant OpenLayers Starter

Welcome to the *Instant OpenLayers Starter*. This book has been especially created to provide you with all of the information that you need to set up OpenLayers. You will learn the basics of OpenLayers, get started with building your first web map, and discover some tips and tricks for using OpenLayers.

This book contains the following sections:

So, what is OpenLayers? explains what OpenLayers actually is, what you can do with it, and why it's so great.

Installation discusses how to download and install OpenLayers with the minimum fuss and then set it up so that you can use it as soon as possible.

Quick start – Creating your first web map shows you how to perform one of the core tasks of OpenLayers; creating web maps. Follow the steps discussed in this section to create your own web map, which will be the basis of most of your work with OpenLayers.

Top features you need to know about illustrates how to perform six tasks with the most important features of OpenLayers. By the end of this section, you will be able to add image and vector overlays, add interaction controls, display attributes information, and build thematic maps using a variety of styles and strategies.

People and places you should get to know provides some community channels and sources for some additional documentations.

So, what is OpenLayers?

OpenLayers is an open source map viewing library, originally developed and released by MetaCarta under a BSD license. It is written in pure JavaScript and makes it easy to incorporate interactive maps from a variety of sources into your web pages and applications. As Christopher Schmidt, one of the main project developers, wrote on the OpenLayers users mailing list:

> *OpenLayers is not designed to be usable out of the box. It is a library designed to help you to build applications, so it's your job as an OpenLayers user to build the box.*

Don't be scared! Building the box could be very easy and fun and this book will show you how! The only two things you actually need to write your code and see it up and running are a text editor and a common web browser. With these tools you can create your Hello World web map, even without downloading anything and writing no more than a basic HTML template and a dozen line of JavaScript code.

Going forward, step-by-step, you will realize that OpenLayers is not only easy to learn but also very powerful. So, whether you want to embed a simple web map in your website or you want to develop an advanced mash-up application by importing spatial data from different sources and in different formats, OpenLayers will probably prove to be a very good choice.

The strengths of OpenLayers are many and reside, first of all, in its compliance with the **Open Geospatial Consortium** (**OGC**) standards, making it capable to work together with all major and most common spatial data servers. This means you can connect your client application to web services spread as WMS, WFS, or GeoRSS, add data from a bunch of raster and vector file formats such as GeoJSON and GML, and organize them in layers to create your original web mapping applications.

From what has been said until now, it is clear that OpenLayers is incredibly flexible in reading spatial data, but another very important characteristic is that it is also very effective in helping you in the process of optimizing the performances of your web maps by easily defining the strategies with which spatial data are requested and (for vectors) imported on the client side. FastMap and OpenLayers make it possible to obtain them!

As we already said at the beginning, web maps created with OpenLayers are interactive, so users can (and want to) do more than simply looking at your creation. To build this interactivity, OpenLayers provides you with a variety of controls that you can make available to your users. Tools to pan, zoom, or query the map give users the possibility to actually explore the content of the map and the spatial data displayed on it. We could say that controls bring maps to life and you will learn how to take advantage from them in a few easy steps.

Fast loading and interactivity are important, but in many cases a crucial aspect in the process of developing a web map is to make it instantly readable. Isn't it useful to build web maps if the users they are dedicated to need to spend too much time before understanding what they are looking at? Fortunately, OpenLayers comes with a wide range of possibilities to styling features in vector layers. You can choose between different vector features, rendering strategies, and customize every aspect of their graphics to make your maps expressive, actually "talking" and—why not?—cool!

Finally, as you probably remember, OpenLayers is pure JavaScript, and JavaScript is also the language of a lot of fantastic **Rich Internet Application** (**RIA**) frameworks. Mixing OpenLayers and one of these frameworks, as we will see later in this book, opens a wide range of possibilities to obtain very advanced and attractive web mapping applications.

Installation

In four easy steps, you will install OpenLayers and start creating your amazing web maps.

Step 1 – What do I need?

OpenLayers is a JavaScript library designed to build web maps, so you must be familiar with the most popular technologies used to create web applications. Basic knowledge of JavaScript and HTML is a prerequisite, while an understanding of CSS is not necessary but convenient.

You can write the recipe's code in a simple text editor, but as an alternative, you may consider an **IDE (Integrated Development Environment)** that provides you with a complete development framework. In this category, we would recommend Aptana Studio 3, an open source, cross-platform IDE with the support for JavaScript, HTML, and CSS. It offers code assist, integrated debugger, and much more. Aptana Studio 3 is available at http://www.aptana.com/products/studio3.

For Windows users, Notepad++ is a very good choice. It is not an IDE, but it is more than a simple text editor and offers syntax highlighting and plugins that are easy to use. It is an open source project, freely available at http://notepad-plus-plus.org.

The authors of this book have adopted the very popular GNU/Linux distribution called Ubuntu as their principal operating system. You may work smoothly even in a Windows or Mac OS X environment, but it would be more comfortable for you to use an Ubuntu system to follow the entire installation process step by step.

If you are unfamiliar with JavaScript, HTML, and CSS, the resources on the Mozilla Developer Network at https://developer.mozilla.org/en/docs/ may be helpful.

You can download Ubuntu at www.ubuntu.com and install it natively on your hard drive as the native operating system, or use a virtual machine such as VirtualBox, available at http://www.virtualbox.org.

Step 2 – Downloading OpenLayers

The latest stable build of OpenLayers is available as a `.tar.gz` or `.zip` archive from the homepage of the project at `http://www.openlayers.org/`. Choose one format and download the latest stable release of the library (2.12 at the time of writing this book).

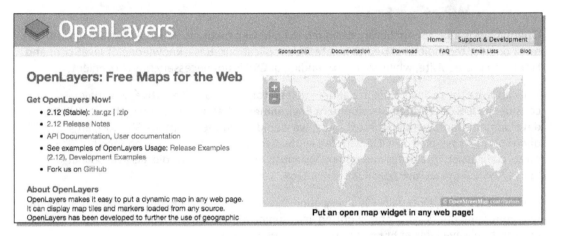

Step 3 – Unpacking OpenLayers

After downloading the archive, you need to unpack it to be left with a directory called `OpenLayers-2.12`, containing a number of files and folders. Now, you just need to create an empty folder in your `/home`, name it `openlayers_starter`, and copy the library into it.

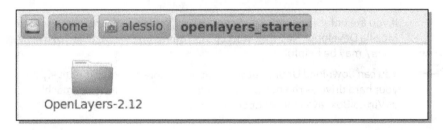

This will be your workspace for all of the recipes and in the next (and last) step we will see where to put it to start having fun with OpenLayers.

Step 4 – Serving the library

OpenLayers is a pure client-side JavaScript library, but in a production environment, JavaScript web applications are distributed through web servers, so it is a good idea to start becoming familiar with this concept. Moreover, in some recipes, we will need to pass a proxy script to retrieve remote data and this requires a web server to be run. So, as final step, you will install and configure a minimal publishing environment on your machine with Apache 2, a very popular open source web server. Its installation in Ubuntu is easy as a pie!

Launch a terminal and type the following into it:

```
~: sudo apt-get install apache2
```

Then, in the same terminal, after the first command finishes, type the following:

```
~: sudo chown -R ${USER} /var/www; ln -s /var/www /home/${USER}/www
```

Let's explain. The first line performs the actual installation. The second line changes the owner of the web server's root directory to your user, and then creates a soft-link to it.

Go to http://localhost with your browser. If the installation succeeds, the Apache 2 web server welcome page opens and displays the message "It works!".

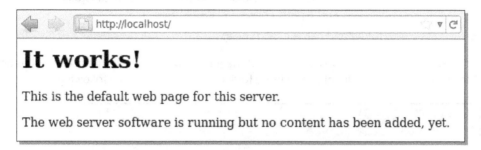

Now, as very last thing, move the openlayers_starter folder into www.

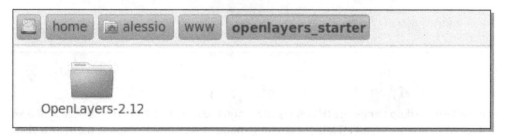

 Windows users can download Apache 2 at http://httpd.apache.org/ and install it in few steps or choose between a number of ready-to-run environments for web development such as BitNami (http://bitnami.org/).

And that's it!

By this point, you should have a working installation of OpenLayers and be free to play around and discover more about it.

Quick start – Creating your first web map

In this section, we will show you how to create your first web map. This Hello World recipe is intended to explain what the key elements to consider are, whenever you want to develop a web map with OpenLayers.

Step 1 – Organizing your workspace

Before starting to write the code, it's a good idea to spend a little time organizing your workspace. Putting everything in order requires just two simple steps:

1. Open the `openlayers_starter` folder created in step 3 of the installation. It should be available at the path `/home/${USER}/www/`.

2. Create a new folder and name it `recipes`.

You just created the folder that will contain all of the recipes we will face until the end of this book. It is at the same level of the OpenLayers library folder as you can see in the following screenshot:

Step 2 – Creating the HTML template

The **HyperText Markup Language** (**HTML**) is the language used to define the structure of a web page. Our web browsers read HTML documents, made of tags, and compose them into visible web pages.

In our case, the purpose of the HTML document we will create is to build the skeleton of the application. It provides OpenLayers with a template that decides where to draw your map once its source code is ready to be executed by the web browser.

Creating your first template is extremely easy:

1. Create an empty file, called `recipe_01.html`, into the `recipes` folder.

2. Using your text editor or IDE, fill the file with the following code:

    ```
    <!DOCTYPE html>
    <html>
      <head>
    ```

```
    <title>Hello World!</title>
    <style>
      #map { width: 800px; height: 600px; }
    </style>
  </head>
  <body>
    <div id="map">
      <!-- The map will be drawn here -->
    </div>
  </body>
</html>
```

Downloading the example code

You can download the example code files for all Packt books you have purchased from your account at http://www.packtpub.com. If you purchased this book elsewhere, you can visit http://www.packtpub.com/support and register to have the files e-mailed directly to you.

3. Save your first HTML template.

Let's explain the template code:

✦ The declaration of the document type at the first line helps the browser to display the web page correctly, while the <html> opening tag, immediately below it, marks the beginning of the HTML template.

✦ The section between the tags <head> and </head> represents the header section of the HTML document. Here we have defined its title using the <title> and </title> tags and a CSS between the tags <style> and </style> to establish the size of the area dedicated to accommodate the map.

✦ The section between <body> and </body> represents the part of the template that the browser translates into the visible elements of the web page. It contains only the div tag <div id="map"></div> which, as explained by the comment inside the code, provides OpenLayers with an area to draw the map. This div tag has an id="map" attribute to make it match the CSS rule about width and height.

✦ Obviously, your HTML template ends with the </html> closing tag.

Step 3 – Including the OpenLayers library

Being a JavaScript library, OpenLayers has to be included in the HTML template to let the browser understand the code written with its classes. The inclusion takes place in the header section, through a reference to the library, using the <script> and </script> tags.

Open your template with the text editor and insert the following line in the header section, just below the title tags, and then save the edits:

```
<script src="../OpenLayers-2.12/OpenLayers.js">
</script>
```

The script opening tag is accompanied by the `src` attribute:

```
src="../OpenLayers-2.12/OpenLayers.js"
```

This references the library by its relative path in the workspace.

At this point, the HTML template knows where OpenLayers is and should look like this:

```
<!DOCTYPE html>
<html>
  <head>
    <title>Hello World!</title>
    <script src="../OpenLayers-2.12/OpenLayers.js"></script>
    <style>
      #map { width: 800px; height: 600px; }
    </style>
  </head>
  <body>
    <div id="map">
      <!-- The map will be drawn here -->
    </div>
  </body>
</html>
```

Step 4 – Defining an initialization JavaScript function

JavaScript code is normally organized in functions, defined as blocks of code delimited by curly braces (`{ }`) and preceded by the `function` keyword. The code inside a function is executed when an event occurs and calls the function.

In this step, we will define a JavaScript function called `initMap` and invoke it by the browser to initialize the map after the page have finished loading. Let's see how:

1. Open your template with the text editor and add the following code below the inclusion of the library:

    ```
    <script type="text/JavaScript">
    function initMap() {

    }
    </script>
    ```

2. Modify the `<body>` opening tag and add an `onload` event attribute to it:

```
<body onload="initMap()">
```

Your updated HTML template should be as follows:

```
<!DOCTYPE html>
<html>
  <head>
    <title>Hello World!</title>
    <script type="text/JavaScript"
      src="../OpenLayers-2.12/OpenLayers.js">
    </script>
    <script type="text/JavaScript">
      function initMap(){

      }
    </script>
    <style>
      #map { width: 800px; height: 600px; }
    </style>
  </head>
  <body onload="initMap()">
    <div id="map">
      <!-- The map will be drawn here -->
    </div>
  </body>
</html>
```

Step 5 – Creating the map

Now that the HTML template is complete, the OpenLayers library is loaded and the initialization function is ready to run, the last step is to write the actual code of our Hello World web map.

In this step, we will meet some terms commonly used in Object Oriented Programming, such as object and constructor. If you are unfamiliar with this paradigm, take a look at this introduction on the Mozilla Developer Network (`https://developer.mozilla.org/en-US/docs/JavaScript/Introduction_to_Object-Oriented_JavaScript`).

In OpenLayers, the `map` object is the first object to instantiate inside the initialization JavaScript function containing the code of your web map. Once a `map` object is defined, it's necessary to add a `layer` object and a series of basic controls to make the map appear and behave according to our desires.

Let's populate the `initMap` function with OpenLayers objects:

1. The first line you need to add will define the variable containing the `map` object. The constructor `new OpenLayers.Map()` takes as argument of the ID of the HTML template element in charge to accommodate the map:

    ```
    var map = new OpenLayers.Map("map");
    ```

2. Proceed with creating an **OpenStreetMap (OSM)** layer object as base layer and add it to the map. The constructor takes a string as first argument, for example, you can use `"Simple OSM BaseMap"`:

    ```
    var osm = new OpenLayers.Layer.OSM("Simple OSM BaseMap");
    map.addLayer(osm);
    ```

3. Define and add a layer switcher control showing a list with the names of layers you added to your map:

    ```
    map.addControl(new OpenLayers.Control.LayerSwitcher());
    ```

4. Define on which part of the Earth's surface your map is centered. Passing a couple of coordinates to the `setCenter` function applied to the map object does the job, but you must also consider the projection. `OpenStreetMap` adopts Web Mercator, so you should pass coordinates in its format to the `LonLat` object. A convenient alternative is to write coordinates in WGS84 (EPSG:4326) and let the OpenLayers transform function do the projection for us. Don't worry, you will be made aware about projections and EPSG codes in the next section. Finally, the number 5 represents the zoom level at start:

    ```
    map.setCenter(
      new OpenLayers.LonLat(10.50, 45.00).transform(
        new OpenLayers.Projection("EPSG:4326"),
        new OpenLayers.Projection("EPSG:900913")
      ),5
    );
    ```

The following is the complete `recipe_01.html` code with the OpenLayers part highlighted:

```
<!DOCTYPE html>
<html>
  <head>
    <title>Hello World!</title>
    <script src="../OpenLayers-2.12/OpenLayers.js"></script>
    <script type="text/JavaScript">
    function initMap(){
      var map = new OpenLayers.Map("map");
      var osm = new OpenLayers.Layer.OSM();
      map.addLayer(osm);
      map.addControl(new OpenLayers.Control.LayerSwitcher());
      map.setCenter(
        new OpenLayers.LonLat(10.50, 45.00).transform(
```

```
          new OpenLayers.Projection("EPSG:4326"),
          new OpenLayers.Projection("EPSG:900913"),
        ),5
      );
    }
    </script>
  </head>
  </body>
    <div id="map">
      <!-- The map will be drawn here -->
    </div>
  </body>
</html>
```

Launch your browser and type the URL of your web map. If you have followed all of the steps properly, it is http://localhost/openlayers_starter/recipes/recipe_01.html.

And the result should be something as the following screenshot:

You just created your first web map. Take some time to play with it, panning and zooming around, and prepare to discover in the next section how easy it is to add features.

Top features you need to know about

In this section, the most common uses of OpenLayers will be shown. You will learn to use external mapping services as base layers for your maps, and to overlay and interact with your own data.

Adding an image overlay

In the previous section, we saw how easy it is to have a basic map with a few lines of code. After creating a `map` object, we are able to fill it with one or more layers that can have a different nature (images and vector data) and be obtained from a plethora of sources. Here we will see how to use layers obtained as images.

Using Google Maps, OSM, and Bing as base layers

In the previous section, we saw how easy it is to have a basic map with a few lines of code. After creating a map object, we are able to fill it with one or more layers that can have a different nature (raster/image and vector data) and be obtained from different kind of sources. In this paragraph, we will focus on image data provided by three of the main third-party map services: Google Maps, Microsoft Bing, and OpenStreetMap. The common feature of these services is that they give access to a set of images (tiles), served by their public web servers, which OpenLayers collects on the basis of our mapping needs (map dimensions, geographical extent, zoom level, and so on) and positions inside our map viewport.

 Google Maps and Microsoft Bing are commercial map services subject to license agreements that do not permit their use for profit, and their free usage is limited to a number of maximum requests per day.

Each of these map services are represented by their own layer type:

✦ `OpenLayers.Layer.Google` for Google Maps
✦ `OpenLayers.Layer.Bing` for Microsoft Bing maps
✦ `OpenLayer.Layer.OSM` for OpenStreetMap

These layers have some common features that we will briefly illustrate.

When set on a `map` object, they are considered by default base layers.

Base layer is an important concept to grasp because OpenLayers gives them prominent importance in managing the way the `map` object and the other layers work together. A base layer is positioned at the base of the layers stack as the background layer, and the `map` object treats it as the "leader" layer, which the other overlay layers obey. For example, the overlay layer's projection must be compatible with the base layer's projection, their geographical extent boundaries are limited by the boundaries set on the base layers, and so on. A map can have only one active base layer while many overlays can be visible at the same time.

Another common denominator for the three types of layers is that the images they refer to maps are projected through a Web Mercator projection, also called as Spherical Mercator, because it treats coordinates as if they were spherical, to simplify computational costs. This is a planar projection, specifically developed for the purposes of World Wide Web mapping services, popularly identified by the code EPSG:900913, extending -180° to 180° W-E, and 85.05113 S and 85.05113 N. These extents allow to visualize a good portion of the Earth with two square images horizontally aligned.

> The **European Petroleum Survey Group (ESPG)** registry is a public dataset of Coordinate Reference Systems. EPSG:900913 is not an official code. It was invented by Google, and the number is a graphical trick where numbers resemble the corporate name. The Spherical Mercator projection was accepted later by EPSG and was assigned the code EPSG:3857.

In the *Quick start* example we wrote the following piece of code:

```
map.setCenter(
  new OpenLayers.LonLat(10.50, 45.00).transform(
    new OpenLayers.Projection("EPSG:4326"),
    new OpenLayers.Projection("EPSG:900913")
  ),5
);
```

Why do we need to transform our lat/lon? If you notice we never said that our map has a EPSG:900913 projection. This follows from the two previous features. The OSM layer is a base layer, so it wants us and the map to consider it as the leader and behave accordingly. Whenever we act on the map, for example, move it, zoom it, click on it, or overlay other layers, we need to obey the base layer's requirements. In this case, we wanted to move the map to a certain position, given in EPSG:4326 lat/lon coordinates, but OSM layer's projection is EPSG:900913. Never try to have words with a base layer. Instead, transform your coordinates as it wishes, and you will get on well with it!

Back to the three layers. Let's see how to set up a Google Map layer. I will add this layer to the map before the OSM layer we set in the previous example.

1. Copy `recipe_02.html` to a new file and name it `recipe_01.html`.

2. Right before the OpenLayers script, add the script for the Google Maps API. This is required to enable OpenLayers to converse with the Google Map service.

   ```
   <script src="http://maps.google.com/maps/api/
   js?v=3&sensor=false"></script>
   ```

3. Create the Google Maps layer:

   ```
   var gs = new OpenLayers.Layer.Google( "Google Satellite", {type:
   google.maps.MapTypeId.SATELLITE, numZoomLevels: 22 );
   ```

4. Add the layer to the map before adding the OSM layer:

    ```
    map.addLayer(gs);
    ```

Expanding the layer switcher, you will be able to change the active base layer. Notice that layer stacking follows the order inside the array used in `map.addLayers()`.

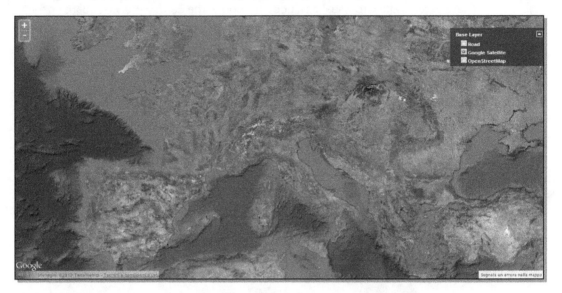

As you will notice, we had to provide some more information compared to the OSM layer. Options are always passed to the layer as a JavaScript literal object (which is defined within curly brackets). In this case we are using two options:

✦ `type`: In the context of a Google Maps layer, we use it to define which kind of Google Maps layer we want to use. These are defined by the Google Maps APIs and include `google.maps.mapTypeId` (`SATELLITE`, `ROADMAP`, `TERRAIN`, and `HYBRID`). They will sound familiar, they're the same as you can switch when navigating to `maps.google.com` and related services.

✦ `numZoomLevels`: This option defines how many zooming levels your map will provide, for example, how much you can zoom in and out, starting from the first zooming level (completely zoomed out). Google Maps ranges from 19 to 22, depending on the type of layer and the geographical zone (some areas have more detailed maps than others), while OSM provides 19 zooming levels.

Zooming is strictly related to map resolution. Zooming levels start from 0, the outmost zoom that can be used on the map. If not otherwise specified, it corresponds to the highest resolution of the layer. The Web Mercator projection uses a spherical model of the Earth whose diameter is about 40075016.68 m, and the services we're treating splits the global map in squared images (tiles) with a 256 px side. Consequently, the zooming level 0 has a resolution of 156543.033906 m/px (40075016.68/256). Each next level is obtained by dividing this value by 2^zoomLevel.

And what about Bing? Simply do the same as for OSM and Google Maps, create the respective layer, and add it to the map.

```
var road = new OpenLayers.Layer.Bing({
        name: "Road",
        key: apiKey,
        type: "Road"
    });
```

The type option is similar to the Google Maps layer. In this case we can use Road, Aerial, and AerialWithLabels. We have one more specific option, key. This is a string that you must obtain from the Bing web portal, to be able to use their Map API.

A final note! Instead of adding the layers one by one, we can group them in one single call to map.addLayers, passing an array with our layers. The first layer will be the default one.

```
map.addLayers([gs,osm,bing]);
```

Using layers from OGC WMS services

Many of you will probably know or have heard about OGC services, WMS and WFS in particular. They are two of the most widely used web map services standards created by the **Open Geospatial Consortium (OGC)**, an international consortium of about 400 companies, government agencies, and universities, which develops public standards in the field of geographical and location-based information systems.

First we'll see **WMS** services, which stands for **Web Mapping Service**. WMS defines a common language to interact between applications and web services to exchange rendered maps in the form of images. The Google Maps service also provides the means to access a repository of maps as images, but it doesn't follow a standard protocol standard interface.

 You can set up your own WMS server. Geoserver and Mapserver are two free map servers which can serve both WMS and WFS services. You can find more information on them on their respective websites. Both of them can also be reached through the open source Geospatial Foundation portal, www.osgeo.org.

OpenLayers provides the `OpenLayers.Layer.WMS` layer type. We will use it to load a thematic geological map of California (USA), published by the **United States Geological Survey (USGS)** map servers. Let's start our new example.

1. Create a new file, `recipe_03.html` as a copy from `recipe_01.html`.

2. Define two WMS layers.

```
var california_litho_lo = new OpenLayers.Layer.WMS(
"California litholohical lo-res map (USGS)", "http://mrdata.usgs.
gov/services/ca",
{layers:"lith-low",transparent:true},
{isBaseLayer:false,projection:"EPSG:900913",maxScale:2370000});

var california_litho_hi = new OpenLayers.Layer.WMS(
"California litholohical hi-res map (USGS)",
"http://mrdata.usgs.gov/services/ca",
{layers:"lith-high",transparent:true},
{isBaseLayer:false,projection:"EPSG:900913",minScale:2370000,opaci
ty:0.5}
);
```

   ° The first parameter to an `OpenLayers.Layer.WMS` is, as usual, the name we want to assign to this layer.

   ° The second one is the URL of the WMS server where our map resides.

   ° The third parameter is an object containing the WMS request options, and must contain at least the name of one map (`layer`) that we want the WMS to serve for. We have added another option to ask the server to supply an image with `transparency` applied on it (null values from the original map layer will make the maps appear transparent, otherwise they will be rendered white).

 Under the hood, OpenLayers asks for a map issuing a `GetMap` request to the WMS server. The complete list of the parameters that can be defined for this type of request are specified by the WMS standard, which is publicly available on the OGC website, `http://www.opengeospatial.org/standards/wms`.

   ° In the OpenLayers's layer options, we have set the projection to be Spherical Mercator, to be compatible with the Google base layer. OpenLayers will ask the WMS server to give back the map projected according to this CRS.

○ In the fourth parameter, we set the layer options. `isBaseLayer` is set to `false` because we want the layer to be shown as an overlay, layered above the base layer. If we didn't set this variable, it would be considered a base layer and we couldn't see it overlayed because, as we said before, only one base layer can be visible at the same time. Finally a scale-related option is used. The two layers should be used alternatively at different scales. The one with low resolution should be used until 1:2370000, then it will be switched off and the one with high resolution will appear. For the high-resolution layer, we also set the layer opacity to 0.5, to make it partially transparent.

We can find all of the information about the available layers, such as CRS and scale constraints (and much more information about the service itself) by issuing a GetCapabilites request as `http://mrdata.usgs.gov/services/ca?request=getcapabilities&service=WMS&version=1.1.1`.

We will obtain an XML response where all of the required information can be retrieved.

3. Add the WMS layers to the map:

```
map.addLayers([gs,california_litho_lo,california_litho_hi]);
```

4. Center the map to an appropriate extent (you can obtain it from the aforementioned `GetCapabilites` request), which creates an `OpenLayers.Bounds`, which represents a rectangular region defined by the lower left corner (minX, minY) and the upper left corner (maxX, maxY) coordinates:

```
var bounds = new OpenLayers.Boun
ds(-125.322,32.4715,-114.205,42.0089).transform( new
OpenLayers.Projection("EPSG:4326"), new OpenLayers.
Projection("EPSG:900913"));

map.zoomToExtent(bounds);
```

5. To prevent the user from panning beyond the defined extent, we can set the `map.restrictedExtent` property to the `bounds` object (notice that it could be set directly as an option when defining the `map` object):

```
map.restrictedExtent = bounds;
```

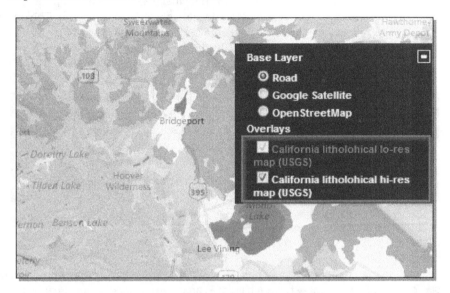

Obtaining information about the mapped features from WMS servers

The OGC WMS specification defines the `GetFeatureInfo` method to obtain information about the features rendered on the map, for example, data attributes. If the layer has the `queryable` attribute set to 1 inside the `GetCapabilites` response, it means you can send a `GetFeatureInfo` request on it.

The `OpenLayers.Control.WMSGetFeatureInfo` object is what we require to perform the request. We will talk about controls later, at this moment it's enough to say that they are objects that let the user interact with the map.

1. Create a new file `recipe_04.html` as a copy of `recipe_02.html`. After the layers' definitions, create the control object:

```
var getFeatureInfo = new OpenLayers.Control.WMSGetFeatureInfo({
  url: 'http://mrdata.usgs.gov/services/ca',
  layers: [california_litho_high, california_litho_high],
    queryVisible:True,
    infoFormat: text/plain
});
```

The URL is the same as the WMS layer, because we are querying the same WMS server.

In layers, we set the array of map layers from which we want to obtain information.

- ° `queryVisible` set to `True` means that we want to perform the `GetFeatureInfo` request only for the layers that are actually visible. In our case, we will obtain information for one layer or the other depending on the actual scale of the map.

- ° `infoFormat` defines the format of the response we want the server to give us back. It is coded as a MIME type, and they are listed in the `GetCapabilities` response. Typical formats are `text/html` for an HTML response, `application/vnd.ogc.gml` for GML, and `text/plain` for simple text. We will use the simpler one, `text`.

2. We define a function that will manage the response from the server. We will simply fire a JavaScript `alert()` to open an information box:

```
function showInfo(response) {
  alert(response.text);
}
```

3. When the control receive a responses from the server, it will signal it to the application by launching a signal, the `getfeatureinfo` event. We want to intercept it and launch the function defined in the previous step:

```
getFeatureInfo.events.register('getfeatureinfo',this,showInfo);
```

4. Let's add the control to the map. We also need to activate it to make it react to the mouse clicks:

```
map.addControl(getFeatureInfo);
getFeatureInfo.activate();
```

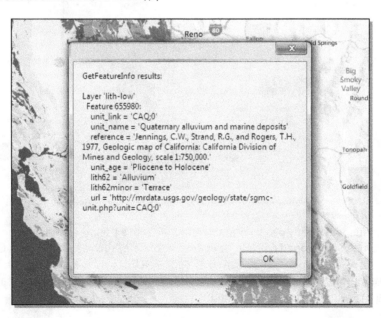

Notice that `GetFeatureInfo` will perform a cross-domain request. We need to set up `proxy.cgi`, as explained earlier in this book, and populate the `OpenLayers.Proxy` property, otherwise no response will be received.

```
OpenLayers.ProxyHost = "/cgi-bin/proxy.cgi?url=";
function initMap(){
   (...)
}
```

Using data from tile servers

The three map providers we used in `recipre_01_gio.html` share a common trait; they all serve the images as a set of tiles of fixed dimension, 256 px wide and 256 px high, each one reachable through its own URL (for example, `http://a.tile.openstreetmap.org/0/0/0.png`). These are, generally, prerendered images kept in a cache to avoid live map rendering. OpenLayers will do several requests to obtain the set of images, which finally will be composed in a continuous, single layer. Tiles are organized in a hierarchical structure, such as a filesystem. Every zooming level (the folder in the filesystem metaphor) has its own set of tiles (the single files), laid in a grid shape where each tile occupies a cell. The tile dimensions are always the same, but starting at minimum zooming level the whole world will be contained in a single tile (refer to the following screenshot), while at the maximum zooming level you may need over a billion tiles to obtain a single image of the earth!

While Google, Bing, and many other commercial services use their own tile scheme, various standards have been developed to define a common scheme, such as WMST from OGC, TMS, WMS-C. Here we will use `OpenLayer.Layer.XYZ`, which provides a generic, configurable scheme. The names recall the tile coordinates; z is the zooming level, and x and y are the coordinates in the grid of tiles for that zooming level.

Beyond public web services such as OpenStreetMap and MapBox, you can use your own map server to publish maps in this fashion. MapProxy and TileStache, for example, are specifically designed to cache and serve tiled maps. Mapserver and Geoserver can also be configured to do this.

Let's see how to load an XYZ layer from a map published through MapBox. Here we will use a base layer, offered out of the box by MapBox, whose source comes from the `NaturalEarth` public domain dataset.

1. Create `recipe_05.html` from `recipe_01.html`. We will only have our new kind of layer, so we can remove the OSM one. Let's define the `XYZ` layer.

    ```
    var earth = new OpenLayers.Layer.XYZ( "Natural Earth",
    ["http://a.tiles.mapbox.com/v3/mapbox.natural-earth-hypso-
    bathy/${z}/${x}/${y}.png"],
    { attribution: "Tiles © MapBox", sphericalMercator: true,
    wrapDateLine: true, numZoomLevels: 19 } );
    ```

    °   The second parameter is an array of URL templates. If multiple URLs are set, OpenLayers will distribute the requests between them, to take advantage of the multiple servers available to collect tiles.

    °   Each URL is a template. This will be used by OpenLayers to craft the request, depending on the tile it requires. If we are viewing the whole Earth from the minimum zooming level, OpenLayers will substitute the variables with $z=0$, $x=0$, and $y=0$.

    °   A template is used because a service could expose a different scheme, for example, with the zooming level of the latter block of the URL ($x/y/z$).

    °   The third parameter is the usual layer option's object. This time we also set an attribution to be shown on the map, and switch on the `wrapDateLine`, which will let us pan in east-west directions indefinitely, passing through the Date Time line (Pacific Ocean), as if we were spinning a globe.

2. Add the layer to the map as usual and center it on China (lon: 110, lat: 35), to a zooming level 4.

To highlight the fact that the map is a composition of a set of square images, 256 px x 256 px, we can add a CSS style class to the `<style>` element of our page, which will override the default one that OpenLayers applies to each tile image and will apply a red border to the tiles.

```
.olTileImage{ border: 1px solid red; }
```

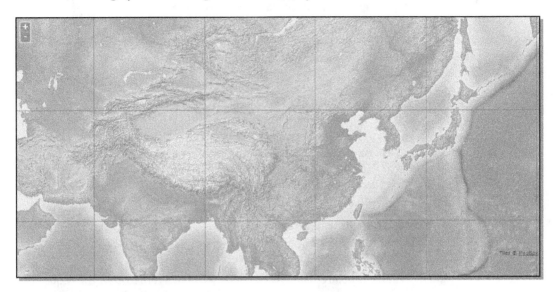

Adding interaction controls

So far we have overlooked the explanation of the `map.addControl` method. We have used it in all our examples and it's time to spend some time on it. It adds `OpenLayers.Control` to the map. There are several kinds of controls available in OpenLayers, which can be roughly subdivided in two broad classes; those that permit you to interact with the map (panning, zooming, selecting features, and so on) and those which provide map widgets and visual information feedback. Here we will only see some of them.

The following basic interaction controls are probably the most widely used:

✦ `OpenLayers.Control.Zoom`: The `map` object uses this control by default. It's the GUI control used to zoom in or zoom out, positioned at top left in the map viewport.

✦ `OpenLayers.Control.PanZoomBar`: This is similar to the zooming control, but it provides visual controls to pan and a slider to step between the zooming levels. In case you want to use this, you should replace the zooming control, because it has the same default position and the two would get overlapped.

✦ `OpenLayers.Control.KeyboardDefaults`: Pans the map with the keyboard arrows.

◆ `OpenLayers.Control.MousePosition`: This stays between interaction and visual control, as it will show geographical coordinates of the current mouse position. The coordinate CRS is the same as the map, but it can be changed by setting the `displayProjection` option on the map:

```
var map = new OpenLayers.Map( "map",{displayProjection:'EP
SG:4326'});
```

Let's see some visual controls now:

◆ `OpenLayers.Control.LayerSwitcher`: This is the only control that we have explicitly used until now. This is the visual widget that shows the layers in the map and lets us switch them on/off.

◆ `OpenLayers.Control.OverviewMap`: A small map will be added at the bottom right of the viewport to show an overview of the current position and extent. By default, it will be a clone of the main map, otherwise we can set specific options and layers for the overview. We could add an overview with the OSM layer only.

◆ `OpenLayers.Control.ScaleLine`: A scale bar will be drawn on the map.

◆ `OpenLayers.Control.Permalink`: This will provide a URL that you can share to let other users land in the same position and zooming level as the current map.

In addition to zoom, another control is added by default to the `map` object, the `OpenLayers.Control.Navigation`. It doesn't have a GUI component, but it provides the invisible mechanism to click-and-drag the map and zoom with the mouse wheel.

Back to our map! We want to enrich it with an overview map, substitute the zoom control with the panzoom control, and add a scale bar.

1. Starting from `recipe_03.html`, create `recipe_06.html`. Controls can be set in one shot during the map creation. We override the default control's array, because we don't want the zoom control to be added. We keep the navigation instead and add the scale bar and the panzoom control. We also set the `LayerSwitcher` here instead of using `map.addControl`.

```
var map = new OpenLayers.Map( "map",{
  controls: [
    new OpenLayers.Control.Navigation(),
    new OpenLayers.Control.PanZoomBar(),
    new OpenLayers.Control.ScaleLine(),
    new OpenLayers.Control.LayerSwitcher()
  ]
});
```

2. Finally, let's create an overview map (which we want maximized when we open the page) with just the OpenStreetMap layer. Instead of creating a brand new OSM layer, we can clone it from the one we already have. Pay attention to not assign the previous OSM layer to a new variable without cloning it!

```
var osm2 = osm.clone();
var overlayOptions = {
  maximized: true,
  layers: [osm2]
};
map.addControl(new OpenLayers.Control.
OverviewMap(overlayOptions));
```

3. This gives a change to the look. Let's rearrange the layer's array in the `map.addLayers` call to set the Bing Maps layer as the default base layer:

```
map.addLayers([bingroad,gs,osm,california_litho_lo,california_
litho_hi]);
```

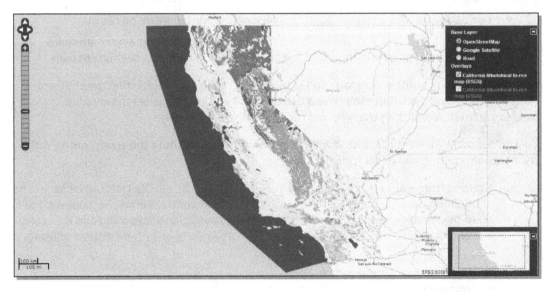

Adding a vector overlay

Technically and in general, a vector layer is an object composed by an array of features, and every feature is an object containing a geometry and an array of attributes.

Vector layers are client side, so once data is downloaded and rendered in your browser, there's no need to send new requests to the server to retrieve information. This characteristic permits a real-time interaction with the features on top of the map, but on the other side, you must be careful in managing large datasets such as vector layers, because they can really slow down things and make your map unusable and unattractive.

With vector layers, we can also create mash-ups, that is, web applications integrating data from external resources and services. An important thing to be aware of is that when we want to populate a vector layer for retrieving information from external web resources, we need to perform cross-domain requests. To be able to retrieve data, we must have set up proxy.cgi, as explained earlier in this book.

Creating a vector layer from GeoJSON data

A vector layer can be added to the map from a variety of sources, as files and web services. In this example, we will see how to create a vector layer based on a GeoJSON file stored on a local folder. Let's go!

1. First of all, take the states.geojson file from the book's code bundle and copy it in your openlayers_starter folder.

The following illustration shows the attributes' structure:

	FID	state_name	e_quakes
0	0	Alaska	1
1	1	Alabama	1
2	2	Arkansas	12
3	3	Arizona	13

This file is a feature collection containing data about the occurrences of earthquakes in the US during the last 30 years. We created this dataset for didactic purpose using information available on the USGS website.

2. Copy recipe_01.html to a new file and name it recipe_07.html.

3. Set the center of the map to United States by changing the coordinates and the zooming level used for the previous recipes.

```
map.setCenter(
new OpenLayers.LonLat(-111.42387,52.41521).transform(
            new OpenLayers.Projection("EPSG:4326"),
            new OpenLayers.Projection("EPSG:900913")
), 3
);
```

4. Just below the OpenStreetMap base layer object code, insert the following lines to create and add the vector overlay on top of the map:

```
var states = new OpenLayers.Layer.Vector("Earthquakes30",{
  protocol: new OpenLayers.Protocol.HTTP({
    url: "../states.geojson",
    format: new OpenLayers.Format.GeoJSON()
  }),
  strategies: [new OpenLayers.Strategy.Fixed()]
});
map.addLayer(states);
```

Let's explain what happened:

◆ We instantiated a new type of layer object, the vector layer. Its constructor, in our snippet, takes the `"Earthquakes 30"` string and two optional parameters between the curly brackets (`{ }`), `protocol` and `strategies`.

◆ The `protocol` parameter takes care of retrieving the data from the source (in this case, it is the GeoJSON file). The `url` and the `format` options respectively specify the data source path and its type.

◆ The `strategies` parameter expects an array of strategy objects that specifies how OpenLayers requests the data. The `Fixed` strategy is a simple strategy that requests features once and never requests new data. We will see other types of strategies in the next paragraphs.

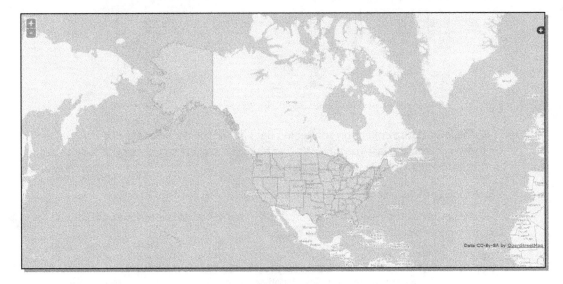

Obtaining vector data from WFS and transforming coordinates with Proj4js

When talking about image-based layers, we have seen the OGC WMS standard. A closely related standard is OGC **WFS**, which stands for **Web Feature Service**. Unlike WMS, it defines a protocol to exchange vector data. We will see `OpenLayers.Protocol.WFS` in action to load a geological layer from the Arizona Geological Survey and overlay it on a Google Maps Satellite base.

The WFS service `GetCapabilities` response lists only one supported CRS, EPSG: 26912. OpenLayers isn't shipped with all of the information and mechanisms to manage the whole range of CRS on the Earth. We have seen that it can transform EPSG:4326 coordinates to EPSG:900913, because they're included by default, but how will we overlay EPSG:26912 geometries on a Google Maps base, which is EPSG:900913?

An external library that helps in this case is `Proj4js`. It is the JavaScript port of a powerful library, `Proj4`, dedicated to CRS transformations and reprojections. `Proj4js` isn't shipped with OpenLayers, but it can cooperate when the former is loaded in our page. We need to download it first from `http://trac.osgeo.org/proj4js/wiki/Download` (the present version is `proj4js-1.1.0.zip`) and extract it inside our web server in the `OpenLayers-2.12` folder.

Let's start our new example.

1. Start `recipe_08.html` from `recipe_02.html` and let's include the `Proj4js` library before the OpenLayers library.

   ```
   <script src="../proj4js/lib/proj4js-compressed.js"></script>
   <script src="../OpenLayers-2.12/lib/OpenLayers.js"></script>
   ```

2. Remove OSM and Bing layers. We will keep a Google Maps layer of the type `SATELLITE`.

3. Now comes the more complicated part, to make `Proj4js` aware of the CRS we need to use. At the very beginning of our script, let's define the CRS as follows:

   ```
   Proj4js.defs["EPSG:26912"] = "+proj=utm +zone=12 +ellps=GRS80
   +datum=NAD83 +units=m +no_defs";
   ```

   What is that? We can't give the details of what that string means, it's beyond the scope of this book, but it is sufficient to say that it's the way to define a CRS in `Proj4`, and in `Proj4js` as a consequence. This particular string represents the EPSG:26912 reference system.

> The Proj4 syntax documentation can be found on the Proj4
> project's site, http://trac.osgeo.org/proj/. You can obtain
> the Proj4 strings for all of the EPSG CRSs from the Spatial
> Reference website, http://spatialreference.org/. As an
> example, the Proj4 definition for EPSG:26912 can be found at
> http://spatialreference.org/ref/epsg/26912/.

OpenLayers will now be able to transform the coordinates to EPSG:900913 coordinates,
so we can superimpose the vectors on OSM, Google Maps, Bing, and so on.

Back to WFS.

1. Let's create the WFS layer representing the railway stations of England.

    ```
    var arizona_geology = new OpenLayers.Layer.Vector("WFS", {
        strategies: [new OpenLayers.Strategy.BBOX()],
        protocol: new OpenLayers.Protocol.WFS({
            url: "http://services.azgs.az.gov/ArcGIS/
            services/GeologicMapOfArizona/MapServer/WFSServer",
            featureType: "Contacts_and_Faults",
            featurePrefix: "GeologicMapOfArizona",
            featureNS:
            "http:///GeologicMapOfArizona/MapServer/WFSServer",
            geometryName: "Shape",
        }),
        projection: new OpenLayers.Projection("EPSG:26912"),
        styleMap: contacts_and_faults
    })
    ```

    The fundamental protocol options are url and featureType, which is the layer we
    are asking for (the WFS standard names it typeName).

    From GetCapabilities, we know that the layer name is prefixed by a
    namespace, that is, GeologicMapOfArizona:Contacts_and_Faults. We add
    featurePrefix to compose the correct typeName. Then we add featureNS,
    which is the URI of the feature namespace and geometryName, that is, the name of
    the geometry column of the data source. These two values can be obtained from a
    DescribeFeatureType request to the WFS server.

    Finally, we define the projection of the layer. It's required to make OpenLayers aware
    that the returned geometries have coordinates according to this CRS.

    In this example, we are using two new elements, OpenLayers.Strategy.BBOX and
    a styleMap parameter (which is defined in the source code of this example). They will
    be introduced later, but in a few words, the first makes OpenLayers download only the
    data for the actual extent of the map and the latter is used to define styling options for
    the layer.

2. Add the layers to the map, centralize the map on the city of Phoenix, and set the zooming level at 11.

```
map.addLayers([osm,os]);
var center = new OpenLayers.LonLat(-112.073889,33.448333).
transform(
   new OpenLayers.Projection("EPSG:4326"),
   new OpenLayers.Projection("EPSG:900913"));
map.setCenter(center,11);
```

 Loading the layer will take a while because the vector geometries are quite detailed, so a lot of data is downloaded. Do not zoom too far, otherwise the data overload could freeze your page!

Adding a vector overlay from GeoRSS

The **GeoRSS** is an OCG standard file format for encoding location as part of a web feed. It would be interesting to use the mash-up approach, because, for example, a GeoRSS source can also be read by common news aggregators (as a normal RSS). An idea would be to use this kind of data source to build a web mapping application that shows a map view and a list of news in the same page. Explaining how to retrieve web feeds in your page is beyond the scope of this book, but there are a bunch of alternatives to accomplish this task (take a look at jFeed, a plugin for the super popular jQuery framework).

There are two encodings for GeoRSS:

✦ **GeoRSS Simple**: Supports basic geometries

✦ **GeoRSS GML (Geography Markup Language)**: Supports a greater range of features than the GeoRSS Simple encoding and coordinate reference systems other than WGS84 latitude/longitude

After this brief introduction, let's prepare our GeoRSS example. In the paragraph about the proxy installation, we added the USGS domain to retrieve remote data from it. In this example, you will learn how to add a GeoRSS source as a vector layer to your map by using the public real-time data that USGS exposes. In our example, we will use GeoRSS Simple for Atom files (available at `http://earthquake.usgs.gov/earthquakes/feed/`).

1. Create a new HTML template, as already shown in the *Quick start* section, and name it `recipe_09.html`.

2. Define your `initMap` function as usual, inside the `script` tag. This time the initialization function has to be preceded by the `OpenLayers.ProxyHost` variable referencing the proxy script on your server:

```
<script >
OpenLayers.ProxyHost = "/cgi-bin/proxy.cgi?url=";

function initMap(){

}
</script>
```

3. Add a `map` object and a base map:

```
var map = new OpenLayers.Map("map");
var osm = new OpenLayers.Layer.OSM("OSM Base Map")
map.addLayer(osm);
```

4. Define and add your GeoRSS-based vector overlay object as follows:

```
var earthquakes = new OpenLayers.Layer.Vector("USGS Feed",{
  protocol: new OpenLayers.Protocol.HTTP({
    url: "http://earthquake.usgs.gov/earthquakes/
    feed/atom/2.5/month",
    format: new OpenLayers.Format.GeoRSS()
  }),
  strategies: [new OpenLayers.Strategy.Fixed()]
});
map.addLayer(earthquakes);
```

As you can see, only the `url` and `format` parameters change compared to the GeoJSON example.

The source in `url` is, obviously, a GeoRSS and the shared real-time data. In this case, consider earthquakes events with a minimum magnitude of 2.5 over the 30 days.

5. Fly to Japan!

```
map.setCenter(
  new OpenLayers.LonLat().transform(
    new OpenLayers.Projection("EPSG:4326"),
    new OpenLayers.Projection("EPSG:900913")
  ), 5
);
```

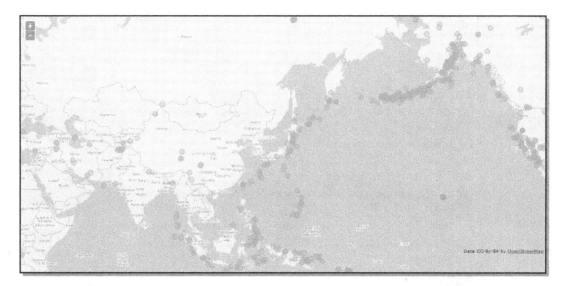

Showing feature attributes in a pop up

An important aspect of GIS is its interactivity, that is, the ability to retrieve information about the elements populating a map. This is true also for web mapping applications and users who, typically, approach them expecting something to happen even before knowing what they are looking for!

OpenLayers provides you with an effective way to build interactivity, and in this example, we will see how to use the selection control and popups to retrieve and show information.

1. Make a copy of the `recipe_10.html` file and name it `recipe_10.html`.

2. Create the selection control below the `map.addLayer(states)` line:

```
var select = new OpenLayers.Control.SelectFeature(states,{
  multiple: false
});
map.addControl(select);
select.activate();
```

Using this code, you add the possibility to select the polygon features of your vector layer (states) by clicking on them. The `multiple:false` option establishes that only one polygon at a time can be selected and the line `selControl.activate()`, of course, makes the new control active and enables it to listen for mouse click events.

3. Add the functions `onSelect` and `onUnselect` to the control constructor:

```
var select = new OpenLayers.Control.SelectFeature(states,{
  multiple: false,
  onSelect: function(feature) {},
  onUnselect: function(feature) {}
});
```

4. Fill in the new functions:

```
var select = new OpenLayers.Control.SelectFeature(states,{
  multiple: false,
  onSelect: function(feature) {
    // Prepare the popup content
    var content = feature.attributes.state_name +": "
    + feature.attributes.e_quakes
    + "Earthquakes in the last 30 years";
    // Create a popup object
    var myPopup = new OpenLayers.Popup.FramedCloud(
      feature.id+"_popup",
      feature.geometry.getBounds().getCenterLonLat(),
      new OpenLayers.Size(150,100),
      content
    );
    // Link the popup to feature and add it to the map
    feature.popup = myPopup;
    map.addPopup(myPopup);
  },
  onUnselect: function(feature) {
    // Remove the popup from map
    map.removePopup(feature.popup);
  }
});
```

Here's what happens:

✦ The `onSelect` function runs when an element on the map is selected and takes the `feature` argument, between round brackets, representing the selected feature object.

✦ The feature object contains the geometry and the attributes. We retrieve the values in `attributes.state_name` and `attributes.e_quakes` for the selected feature and store them into the `content` variable.

✦ The variable called `myPopup` contains the pop-up object. The arguments passed to the `OpenLayers.Popup.FramedCloud` subclass constructor include the ID, a string that identifies the specific pop-up, the location where the pop-up must appear, the pop-up size in pixels, and our `content` variable with the information in the form of an HTML string.

✦ The last two lines inside the `onSelect` function relate the pop-up to the current feature, and finally, display it on the map.

✦ The `onUnselect` function is executed when a feature is unselected. The argument is the unselected feature and it is passed to the `removePopup` function.

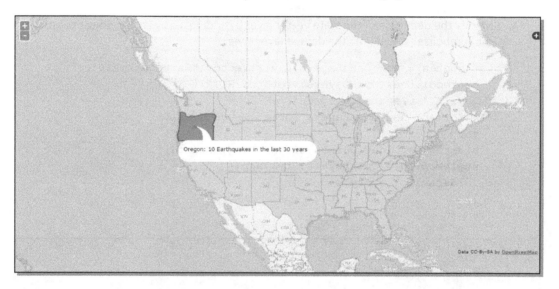

Creating a thematic map

In this section, you will learn how to create a thematic map by using the OpenLayers styling capabilities.

A **thematic map** focuses on a specific theme or subject area, whereas in a general map the variety of phenomena—such as geological, geographical, and political—regularly appear together. The contrast between them lies in the fact that thematic maps use the base data, such as coastlines, boundaries, and places, only as points of reference for the phenomenon being mapped.

First of all, we will use the `StyleMap` and `Style` classes to customize the graphic appearance of the features.

1. Make a copy of the `recipe_09.html` file and name it `recipe_11.html`.

2. Define the `myStyle` variable just before the state vector layer definition to create a `Style` object. It consists of a symbolizer with a `key:value` pair, similar to CSS:

```
var myStyle = new OpenLayers.Style({
  fillColor: '#CC3333',
  fillOpacity: .75,
  strokeColor: '#FFF',
  strokeWidth: 2
});
```

3. Modify the definition of the state vector layer by adding a `styleMap` object to apply the symbolizer, and define the default layer style:

```
var states = new OpenLayers.Layer.Vector("Earthquakes30",{
  protocol: new OpenLayers.Protocol.HTTP({
    url: "../states.geojson",
    format: new OpenLayers.Format.GeoJSON()
  }),
  strategies: [new OpenLayers.Strategy.Fixed()],
  styleMap: new OpenLayers.StyleMap({
    'default': myStyle
  })
});
```

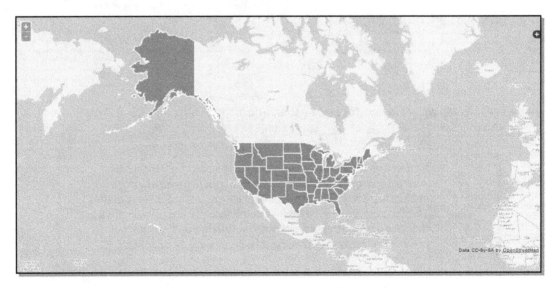

What we've just seen is a very basic styling example, but obviously we can do much more. In the next example, thanks to the `Rule` and `Filter` classes, we will explain how to style features depending on the values stored into their attributes:

1. Make a copy of the `recipe_11.html` and name it `recipe_12.html`.

2. Let's define some rules just before the `myStyle` object:

```
// match e_quakes values equal to 0
var equalTo_rule = new OpenLayers.Rule({
  filter: new OpenLayers.Filter.Comparison({
    type: OpenLayers.Filter.Comparison.EQUAL_TO,
    property: 'e_quakes',
    value: 0
  }),
  symbolizer: { fillColor:'#CCC' }
});

// match e_quakes values between 1 and 10
var between_rule = new OpenLayers.Rule({
  filter: new OpenLayers.Filter.Comparison({
    type: OpenLayers.Filter.Comparison.BETWEEN,
    property: 'e_quakes',
    lowerBoundary: 1,
    upperBoundary: 10
  }),
  symbolizer: { fillColor: '#F60' }
});

// match e_quakes values greater than 10
var greaterThan_rule = new OpenLayers.Rule({
  filter: new OpenLayers.Filter.Comparison({
    type: OpenLayers.Filter.Comparison.GREATER_THAN,
    property: 'e_quakes',
    value: 10
  }),
  symbolizer: { fillColor: '#FF0000' }
});
```

Each rule consists of:

- `filter` used to specify a condition
- `symbolizer` that applies certain graphic properties if the specified condition occurs

In particular, in this example, we have three comparison filters looking for the values stored in the e_quakes attribute of the states vector layer. When the current value is EQUAL_TO, BETWEEN, or GREATER_THAN, the value expected by the filter, the consistent symbolizer is used, and the feature is styled subsequently.

3. Now that you have a group of rules, the last step is adding them to your original myStyle object as an array:

```
var myStyle = new OpenLayers.Style({
  fillColor: '#CC3333',
  fillOpacity: .75,
  strokeColor: '#FFF',
  strokeWidth: 2
},{
  // Apply rules
  rules:[ equalTo_rule, between_rule, greaterThan_rule ]
});
```

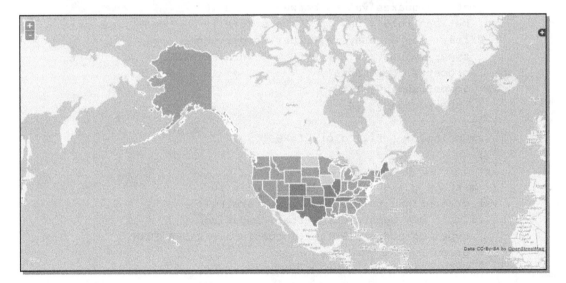

Using strategies and attribute replacement

At the beginning of this book we said that it is important to make our web maps easy to understand for users and as fast as possible. We looked at styles, rules, and filters objects, now we will introduce the strategy class that is responsible for how OpenLayers requests remote data and what it does with the returned features.

We have already used `Strategy.Fixed` in the previous examples, now we will introduce the `Strategy.BBOX` and `Strategy.Cluster` classes:

✦ `Strategy.Fixed`: As you may remember, this class requests for data once and never again.

✦ `Strategy.BBOX`: This class requests for data within the visible extent of the map. It is usually adopted to retrieve WFS data and it is particularly advantageous when you are working with a lot of feature. Note that it does not take effect if applied to static sources as, for example, GeoJSON local files.

✦ `Strategy.Cluster`: This class is applicable to point features and tells OpenLayers to group them on the basis of their distance in pixels before drawing them. This strategy needs to be combined with other fixed or BBOX strategies that are specifically in charge to retrieve data.

Fixed, BBOX, and cluster are part of the available strategy classes. If you want to learn more about strategies and see them in action, visit the OpenLayers official website and explore the examples page available at http://openlayers.org/dev/examples/

In the next example, we will combine the `Strategy.BBOX` and `Strategy.Cluster` classes. This is a solution that could actually save you when working with vector layers . It containing tons of point features and maintaining your web map responsive and easy to read. Moreover, this strategy combo can be used to obtain very expressive representations through a simple but powerful feature called attributes replacement. It is achieved by defining a `context` object inside the `OpenLayers.Style` object specified for your vector layer.

If you look at the previous example's map, what you see could be a little confusing! There are areas in which points representing earthquakes overlap each other and it is difficult to understand what is happening. Let's clarify things!

1. Make a copy of `recipe_12.html` and name it `recipe_13.html`.

2. Modify your GeoRSS vector layer definition by substituting the fixed strategy with the BBOX one and adding the cluster strategy in the `strategies` array. The changes are shown in the following code snippet:

```
var earthquakes = new OpenLayers.Layer.Vector("USGS Feed",{
  protocol: new OpenLayers.Protocol.HTTP({
  url: "http://earthquake.usgs.gov/earthquakes/
  feed/atom/2.5/month",
    format: new OpenLayers.Format.GeoRSS()
  }),
  strategies: [
    new OpenLayers.Strategy.Fixed(),
    new OpenLayers.Strategy.Cluster()
  ]
});
```

3. Try to run `recipe_14.html` in the browser and note that the map is cleaner. The reason, as you may easily realize, is that point features are no longer represented one by one, but they are aggregated and drawn as clusters:

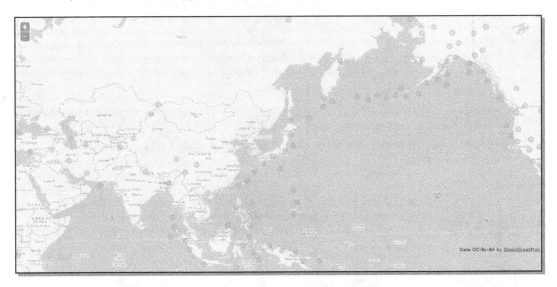

4. Now your web map looks clean, but its informative value is very low because it is not possible to understand, at a glance, how many points are included in each cluster. We need to take profit from a style object based on a custom function taken as value of a `context` object:

```
var earthquakes = new OpenLayers.Layer.Vector("USGS Feed",{
  protocol: new OpenLayers.Protocol.HTTP({
    url: "http://earthquake.usgs.gov/earthquakes/
    feed/atom/2.5/month",
    format: new OpenLayers.Format.GeoRSS()
  }),
  strategies:[
    new OpenLayers.Strategy.Fixed(),
    new OpenLayers.Strategy.Cluster()
  ],
  styleMap: new OpenLayers.StyleMap({
    'default': new OpenLayers.Style({
      fillColor:'#CC3333',
      strokeColor:'#FFF',
      graphicName:'circle',
      fontColor:'#FFF',
      fontSize:'10',
      pointRadius:'${radiusFn}',
      label:'${labelFn}'
```

```
    },{ context: {
      radiusFn:function(features){
        var fc = features.attributes.count;
        if (fc == 1){
          return 6;
        } else if ((fc>1)&&(fc<25)){
          return 10;
        } else if ((fc>25)&&(fc<100)){
          return 12;
        } else {
          return 15;
        }
      },
      labelFn:function(features){
        var fc = features.attributes.count;
          if (fc > 1){
            return fc;
          } else {
            return '';
          }
        }
      }
    })
  })
});
```

5. Run the example again in your browser and try to navigate and zoom to see how clusters explode and implode depending on the zooming level:

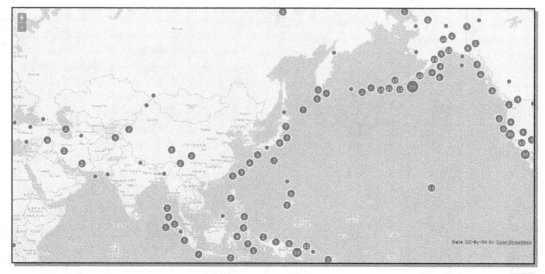

Let's explain what happened:

+ First of all, we added a `styleMap` object to the vector layer and specified a default `Style` object with some attributes. Just to show you an alternative, this time we created the style directly into the vector layer definition (in a different way than what we used for the thematic map's example).

+ Among the `Style` object's properties, two are valorised by using an attribute replacement function:

```
pointRadius:'${radiusFn}',
label:'${labelFn}'
```

+ The `context` object, specified as an optional parameter of the `Style` object, hosts the `radiusFn` and `labelFn` functions. These functions take the features as arguments and return, respectively, a proper value for the radius and the label properties of each cluster on your web map. In this case, the attribute we consider is the number of points (earthquakes) clustered together.

People and places you should get to know

As other free projects, OpenLayers is also characterized by a very active and open community of users and developers. Beyond the access to the source code, a lot of documentation, tips, and user recipes can be found at the official website and the various community channels.

Official site and documentation

+ **Site**: http://openlayers.org/

+ **Documentation and Wiki**: http://trac.openlayers.org/wiki/Documentation

+ **Blog**: http://openlayers.org/blog

+ **Code repository**: https://github.com/openlayers/openlayers

+ **Examples**: http://dev.openlayers.org/releases/OpenLayers-2.12/examples/

Community channels

+ **Official mailing list**: http://trac.osgeo.org/openlayers/wiki/MailingLists

+ **Official IRC channel**: irc://irc.freenode.net/#openlayers

+ **User recipes**: http://trac.osgeo.org/openlayers/wiki/UserRecipes

+ **User FAQs**: http://trac.osgeo.org/openlayers/wiki/ FrequentlyAskedQuestions

About Packt Publishing

Packt, pronounced 'packed', published its first book "*Mastering phpMyAdmin for Effective MySQL Management*" in April 2004 and subsequently continued to specialize in publishing highly focused books on specific technologies and solutions.

Our books and publications share the experiences of your fellow IT professionals in adapting and customizing today's systems, applications, and frameworks. Our solution based books give you the knowledge and power to customize the software and technologies you're using to get the job done. Packt books are more specific and less general than the IT books you have seen in the past. Our unique business model allows us to bring you more focused information, giving you more of what you need to know, and less of what you don't.

Packt is a modern, yet unique publishing company, which focuses on producing quality, cutting-edge books for communities of developers, administrators, and newbies alike. For more information, please visit our website: www.packtpub.com.

Writing for Packt

We welcome all inquiries from people who are interested in authoring. Book proposals should be sent to author@packtpub.com. If your book idea is still at an early stage and you would like to discuss it first before writing a formal book proposal, contact us; one of our commissioning editors will get in touch with you.

We're not just looking for published authors; if you have strong technical skills but no writing experience, our experienced editors can help you develop a writing career, or simply get some additional reward for your expertise.

OpenStreetMap

ISBN: 978-1-84719-750-4   Paperback: 252 pages

Be your own cartographer

1. Collect data for the area you want to map with this OpenStreetMap book and eBook

2. Create your own custom maps to print or use online following our proven tutorials

3. Collaborate with other OpenStreetMap contributors to improve the map data

Instant Google Map Maker Starter

ISBN: 978-1-84969-528-2   Paperback: 50 pages

Learn what you can do with Google Map Maker and get started with building your first map

1. Learn something new in an Instant! A short, fast, focused guide delivering immediate results

2. Understand the basics of Google map maker

3. Add places of interest such as your hotels, cinemas, schools, and more

4. Edit and update details for existing places

Please check **www.PacktPub.com** for information on our titles

OpenLayers Cookbook

ISBN: 978-1-84951-784-3   Paperback: 300 pages

60 recipes to create GIS web applications with the open source JavaScript library

1. Understand the main concepts about maps, layers, controls, protocols, events etc

2. Learn about the important tile providers and WMS servers

3. Packed with code examples and screenshots for practical, easy learning

OpenLayers 2.10 Beginner's Guide

ISBN: 978-1-84951-412-5   Paperback: 372 pages

Create, optimize, and deploy stunning cross-browser web maps with the OpenLayers JavaScript web-mapping library

1. Learn how to use OpenLayers through explanation and example

2. Create dynamic web map mashups using Google Maps and other third-party APIs

3. Customize your map's functionality and appearance

4. Deploy your maps and improve page loading times

Please check **www.PacktPub.com** for information on our titles

www.ingramcontent.com/pod-product-compliance
Lightning Source LLC
Chambersburg PA
CBHW060442060326
40690CB00019B/4298